A SERIES TO REMEMBER

"You can't describe it. You can't put it into words. It's baseball!"
—Joe Carter

WOODFORD PRESS, *San Francisco*
Produced in partnership with
MAJOR LEAGUE BASEBALL PROPERTIES INC.

AN OFFICIAL PUBLICATION OF MAJOR LEAGUE BASEBALL

1993 World Series

A SERIES TO REMEMBER

A SERIES TO REMEMBER
Toronto and Philadelphia, 1993

CREATIVE DIRECTOR AND DESIGNER
Laurence J. Hyman

EDITOR
Jon Rochmis

PHOTOGRAPHY EDITOR
Dennis Desprois

ASSOCIATE ART DIRECTOR
Jim Santore

MARKETING DIRECTOR
David Lilienstein

ASSISTANT DESIGNER
Todd Everett

EDITORIAL ASSISTANTS
McLean Brice
Kate Hanley
Bret Hofstein
Neil Rabin

PHOTOGRAPHERS
Stephen Green (crew chief)
Jon Blacker
Beth Hansen
David Lilienstein
Mark O'Neill
Mickey Palmer
Rosemary Rahn
Jerry Wachter
Jon Winet
Michael Zagaris

WRITERS
Joe Morgan
Buck Martinez
Jon Rochmis

Produced in partnership with and licensed by
MAJOR LEAGUE BASEBALL PROPERTIES, INC.

DIRECTOR OF PUBLISHING
Michael Bernstein

SUPERVISOR, PUBLISHING
Cynthia McManus

ADMINISTRATOR, PUBLISHING
Dana Nicole Williams

ASSISTANT, PUBLISHING
Jennifer Langness

MAJOR LEAGUE BASEBALL®

This book was made possible with the generous assistance of Starter Corporation
STARTER®

WOODFORD PRESS
660 Market Street ● San Francisco, California 94104

All photographs appearing in *A SERIES TO REMEMBER* were shot exclusively on Film.

ISBN: 0-942627-19-9

Library of Congress Catalog Number: 93-61703

First Printing: December 1993

PRINTED AND BOUND IN THE UNITED STATES OF AMERICA

INTRODUCTION

by Buck Martinez

I T DIDN'T RATE AS anything more than a mention in small type on the sports pages on May 10, 1981 when the Toronto Blue Jays traded outfielder Gil Kubski to the Milwaukee Brewers for me. It wasn't exactly the type of deal general managers spend hours working on in back rooms, and it certainly didn't jolt the Toronto sporting community.

The first time I ran down to the bullpen at old Exhibition Stadium, a fan hollered, "Are you the new bad catcher?"

Actually, he was asking if I were the "back catcher," which is the Canadian term for "catcher." They also called my mitt a Decker.

Soon after my arrival we played the Baltimore Orioles on Touque (rhymes with kook) Day. A touque is French for sock hat. A touque with a Blue Jays logo on it was one of the most prized possessions among Canadian sports fans.

With my trusty Decker, I played back catcher for the Toronto Blue Jays from 1981 through 1986. Let me amend that by saying I was a back-up back catcher. On cold days when I didn't play, at least I had my touque.

Baseball was certainly a different experience in Toronto. At the time, I couldn't possibly have known that the Blue Jays would soon set the performance standard for all Major League Baseball franchises.

I never got to play in a World Series, which will always leave a void in my life. When a man becomes a professional ballplayer, there is no greater dream than winning a World Series—much less playing in one. The opportunity to be recognized as the best is what pushes each player.

The Blue Jays didn't act very excited when they defeated the Chicago White Sox for the American League pennant. Devon White replied, "We are excited, but we know we have another step to take. Many people didn't think we had enough heart to push ourselves again, or that we couldn't overcome the loss of so many players off last year's team. We knew inside that we could repeat, and that was our goal."

The Phillies had a similar resolve, but it came from a different mindset. If the Blue Jays were "the best team money could buy," the Phillies were a group of castoffs and misfits. They had finished last in their division in 1992, and to say they were written off for 1993 is inaccurate because it implies they were considered contenders to begin with. But they had developed a special chemistry early in Spring Training, and it carried them through the tough times in September.

The 1993 World Series was special for me because it involved the first organization I played with and the last. I had signed with the Phillies in 1967 out of Sacramento City College because some of my friends were already in the organization and I thought we could all go to the big leagues together. John Vukovich and I played American Legion Baseball together, frequently against a shortstop named Larry Bowa.

To be in the Phillies organization—or to be a fan—is probably not unlike being associated with the Chicago Cubs or Boston Red Sox. There's such wonderful tradition and history. There's also tremendous frustration and angst. "Phillies" is the oldest team nickname in the National League, and Philadelphia was actually in the National League before any other franchise now playing. Yet the Phillies have won just one World Championship in 111 years.

There was a tremendous irony in the 1993 World Series. In an attempt to change the team's image as chronic losers, Phillies officials in 1944 staged a contest to rename the team. The winner was "Blue Jays," and that's how they were informally known for two years. It didn't change anything in the standings, though.

Throughout the stretch drive of 1993, the bitter memories of 1964—when the Phillies blew the pennant in the last week of the season—were replayed day after day. Many fans this year initially were hesitant to make the emotional commitment, lest they be let down once again.

How little a Phillies fan must relate to a Blue Jays fan! Toronto's first season in the American League was in 1977, and already the Blue Jays have won two World Championships.

Some outsiders think Toronto fans are a little blasé because there's a feeling they expect a post-season every year. The fans' reputation comes so much from the stadium where they play, the palatial SkyDome. It's air-conditioned, with a luxury hotel, trendy bars, a gourmet candy stand in the concourse, a big scoreboard high above centerfield. During the seventh-inning stretch, it's the largest aerobics class in the world. The fans enjoy the surroundings, wait to be entertained and usually go home happy.

Then there's Philadelphia, where Veterans Stadium is a no-nonsense facility for its meat-and-potatoes fans, a place where the people can get close to the players and let them know exactly how they feel. These fans have been accused of booing the Easter Bunny and Mother's Day—but there has never been a more sincere, cathartic, satisfied sound than their cheers after the Phillies won the National League pennant. It was just as loud after Curt Schilling's sensational shutout in Game Five, which sent the Series back to Toronto.

Blue Jays fans have been known to cheer just as loudly, and then parade by the hundreds of thousands—peacefully—down Yonge Street.

Many experts made the Blue Jays overwhelming favorites to win the 1993 World Series, as if Toronto had caught some kind of break in playing the Phillies. The Braves, after all, with their "Rolls Royce" starting rotation and beefed-up offense, were the team to be feared. But the Phillies beat them in six games for the well-deserved right to play for the World Championship.

Maybe the Phillies didn't look as clean-cut and coifed as the Blue Jays, but this was not a fashion show.

And what great baseball it was. We witnessed the highest scoring game in World Series history, the greatest clutch hit in World Series history and one of the gutsiest pitching performances in World Series history. Six great games, two great teams.

To them, I tip my touque.

Joe Morgan was inducted into the Baseball Hall of Fame in 1990 following a brilliant 22-year major league career. Since his retirement he has been a highly respected baseball analyst for ESPN.

THE WORLD SERIES IN SIX ACTS

by Joe Morgan

T HE WORLD SERIES is a huge stage that grows much larger beginning with the fourth or fifth game. Players are so thrilled to have advanced to the pinnacle of the baseball season that for the first two or three games everything is easy, a joyride. A team can't be eliminated in the first game, so the intense pressure to perform at a supreme level hasn't yet developed.

The players start to wake up when they start running out of games. They realize this is for real, this is all that's left, this is for the World Championship. They start to play a little differently. It's rare for a rookie or a second-year player to perform at his best in a situation like that. Stage fright isn't unusual. It happens to rookies and veterans alike. That's why it's so impressive for a ballplayer to play at his best in a World Series, when he takes the stage and isn't intimidated by it.

The World Series demands that you be the right guy at the right time.

When people look back at the 1993 World Series, they'll remember Joe Carter was the right guy at the right time.

Carter's home run off Mitch Williams in the bottom of the ninth of the sixth game was a great moment in sports history. It was the first time that a home run overcame a deficit and ended a World Series. Carter's turn came up and he did something special with it. The fans at SkyDome that night were very lucky to have experienced the moment.

But Joe Carter only delivered the game-winning hit. He didn't beat Philadelphia and win the World Series for Toronto by himself. Without so many other great individual performances, without other people taking advantage of their moment on the stage, Joe Carter wouldn't have had the opportunity that Little Leaguers only dream about.

There were so many things that, in the end, made the 1993 World Series special and historic. We saw Lenny Dykstra at his absolute best. The same for Roberto Alomar, Devon White, Paul Molitor, Curt Schilling, Duane Ward. Milt Thompson came through when the Phillies needed it. These players stepped up to the stage and delivered. We'll remember them, just as we remember every player who made a name for himself in a World Series.

13

The 1993 World Series also stood out as a testament to Cito Gaston's greatness as a manager. It remains uncertain how history will record his managerial career, but it is a fact that the last manager to win two straight World Championships before Gaston was one of the greatest managers of all time, Sparky Anderson, who won two straight with Cincinnati in 1975-76. Yet Gaston was the object of so much criticism from many fans and media members all year. Criticism is part of baseball, but what doesn't make sense is that Gaston was almost an afterthought in Manager of the Year balloting.

Perhaps the critics don't like Cito's style as a manager, his mellow demeanor, the apparent inconsistency of his decisions. But this era demands a different kind of manager. The chore of handling players is different. The economics of the game and the nature of the players have made managers so much more important than they were before the 1980s.

In addition to having a great baseball mind, Cito has the perfect temperament to be a manager. He treats his players as individuals, he manages according to the situation, and he gets the most out of his team. Not every move he made in the 1993 World Series was perfect, but time will show that he managed his team as well as it could be managed.

Jim Fregosi also did an excellent job of managing. His style is different than Cito's—he's more demonstrative—but it was extremely effective with the group of players he had. The Phillies weren't the most talented team in the National League in 1993; they finished last in their division in 1992 and didn't make wholesale changes to their basic lineup. They won the pennant because Fregosi knew his team. He managed his players according to their capabilities, he knew they would play hard, and he let his guys play. Even Lenny Dykstra admitted before the Series was over that Toronto had more talent. But Dykstra also said having more talent didn't guarantee the Blue Jays would win. He was saying the Blue Jays were going to have to play their best to beat the Phillies, because the Phillies were going to play their best.

That's exactly what happened.

The Blue Jays received so much criticism for "buying" the pennant. No team can buy a pennant, just as a person can't buy love or happiness. A team can buy talent, but it still has to do something with that talent. Toronto had to replace half its roster after winning the 1992 World Series. Only 13 players from the 1992 team returned in 1993, and some of the players they lost were key people, like Dave Winfield, Jimmy Key, David Cone, Kelly Gruber. There was considerable discussion about the great sums of money the Blue Jays spent, but they spent it *wisely*. The Blue Jays spent their money on Molitor, Dave Stewart, Rickey Henderson, Tony Fernandez. Those transactions showed that their general manager, Pat Gillick, knew what his team needed and that Gaston knew how to put it together.

Spending a lot of money isn't a negative. It's a positive if it's done right, by buying quality and then utilizing it in the most productive way.

The Blue Jays have always had a pretty good gauge on trends in the game. The front office, specifically Pat Gillick, looked at what was happening around the major leagues. Gillick realized that in 1993, more than any other year, a team could hit its way to a championship, and that's how he went about setting up the team.

At one time, great pitching and defense would be enough to win a championship, but there hasn't been great overall pitching in the 1990s. Atlanta and Baltimore had great pitching, but they didn't win their pennants. There are so many great young hitters around now—Ken Griffey, Juan Gonzalez, Barry Bonds, Frank Thomas, Albert Belle, David Justice—but the same proportion of great young pitchers doesn't exist.

Someday the cycle will change. But if pitching is 80 percent of the game, as the experts say it is, why did Toronto win, and why did the Phillies win? It's because 1993 was the year a team could win the championship by outscoring its opponents.

Great pitching will always stop good hitting and even great hitting, but merely good pitching will not stop great hitting. A team can never have enough good pitching; in fact, the Blue Jays tried to add another pitcher to their staff before the trading deadline in September. They were unable to do it. Instead, they went the other way and built up their offense by signing Rickey Henderson. If a team wants to improve itself and can't take half a run away from its opposition, it should add half a run to the offense.

A short series—specifically, the World Series—produces a different dynamic. If one pitcher gets hot, he can dominate and put his team in a position to win it all. Had Curt Schilling pitched a first game like his second game, when he went the distance to shut out Toronto, the Series might have turned out differently. Therefore, what he did in Game Five made him a little more special for the stage. He showed he can handle the moment.

It's important to recognize how well Schilling did his job, first in shutting down the Braves in the NLCS, then doing the same thing to Toronto the day after the 15-14 game. The Phillies could easily have folded after losing that game. Instead, behind Schilling, they shut out a team that had scored 37 runs in the first four games. The Blue Jays scored 45 runs in six games—an average of almost 7.5 runs per game—and that includes being shut out once! Curt Schilling is a bulldog, and he should always be remembered favorably for what he did in the 1993 post-season.

The Phillies' only chance to beat the Blue Jays was in a low-scoring Series. The Blue Jays were more capable of coming from behind than Philadelphia because they had more power. They also knew how to come from behind. That was part of their makeup and personality, both of which came from their manager. Teams are extensions of their manager. Gaston never panicked even when things weren't going well. He stayed calm; therefore, the players stayed calm. Players tend to panic with a manager who jumps up and runs around. That's one of the reasons the Blue Jays were such a good comeback team, because they

didn't panic. In Game Four, they came back twice from a 5-run deficit and won 15-14 on the road. That showed the character of the Blue Jays' team—a disposition Gaston helped establish through his approach to the game and his players.

Game Four was one of those games where the hitting was contagious, although it's rare for that to happen to both teams. Another rarity: The Blue Jays won the highest scoring game in World Series history, on the road at Veterans Stadium, and they did not hit a home run. That's the ultimate in team baseball, getting a hit and driving them in, getting a hit and driving them in.

Toronto's style provides a noticeable contrast between the two teams. The Blue Jays were methodical, the Phillies hot and cold. The Phillies may have led in Game Four most of the way, but it's only because they hit three big home runs. Usually, hitting like that is enough to get the job done, except in this Series.

Gaston's use of Paul Molitor in Games Three and Four was one of the most controversial subjects during the Series. When the Series moved to the National League park, there was no designated hitter rule. Molitor was the the Blue Jays' designated hitter and they needed his right-handed bat in the lineup. Defensively, Molitor was considered capable of playing only one position, first base, but that was John Olerud's position—and Olerud had just captured the American League batting crown. Molitor had played third in his career, but not regularly since 1989. Plus, he had a sore shoulder, limiting his throwing, and it would have been too risky to put him there. Gaston had a big decision to make.

In Game Three, the Phillies sent out Danny Jackson, a left-hander. Gaston's choices were to put Molitor on the bench and have him available to pinch hit later on, keeping Olerud at first and Ed Sprague at third. Or he could have benched Olerud and used Molitor at first. The riskiest choice was to play Molitor at third in place of Sprague.

Gaston's decision wasn't much of a surprise. He played Molitor at first because Olerud is a left-handed hitter. Even though Olerud hit left-handers well, Molitor was a stronger hitter against left-handers. Molitor went 3-for-4, hit a home run and a triple and scored three times, and also made a pretty good play on defense.

It was interesting that some people still were prepared to castigate Cito for benching Olerud if Molitor had cost Toronto the game. Even Dave Stewart said during the Series, "I've never seen a manager get second-guessed as much as Cito Gaston, especially a manager who wins."

It couldn't possibly have been easy for Gaston to decide to bench the league batting champion. The team's reaction to the decision reflected its commitment to Cito. Nobody whined, nobody complained. That's because he treated all his players as individuals, but the team always came first. Gaston was severely criticized for taking so many Toronto players to the 1993 All-Star Game, but his action was a message to his players, showing his support and respect for them. That can't help but foster team unity. He was looking out for his team. Still, he got vilified for it, even though the bottom line always should be to win, and the American League won that game.

In Game Four, Gaston had the same problem of playing with no DH, but the Phillies' pitcher was a right-hander, Tommy Greene. It was natural to return Olerud to first, but Cito also changed his mind about Molitor and started him at third. The reason was simple: Gaston looked at his team and said to himself, "Which nine guys give us the best chance of winning?" Obviously, Molitor was one of those guys, so Cito found a place for him.

Something else undoubtedly went into his decision: It's easier to play third base on artificial surface, because the bounce is truer. If this game had been played in Atlanta, or some other stadium with real grass, Molitor probably would not have been at third.

Nothing is etched in stone with Gaston, which perhaps irritates a few people from the old school. Gaston doesn't always do things by the book. But that book was written in 1910 or 1920, and it doesn't take into account the fact that the game changes. Just because Casey Stengel bunted in a certain situation in the 1950 World Series doesn't mean every manager has to bunt in the same situation every time.

Every game is different, so there should never be one set of rules. Games may be similar to one another, but no two can be exactly alike, if only because pitchers change every day. Therefore, the speed, the pace of the game will change from day to day. There were six World Series games in 1993, and not one of them was alike, even though the same basic line-up went out every game. Managers such as Cito do things according to what they feel at the time. That's how a manager *should* manage.

The Phillies made it a great Series. The Phillies were an easy team to like and they were a fun team to watch because they came out playing hard right from the start and played hard all season long. That's a tribute to all the players and to Fregosi because the Phillies had finished last in their division the year before. In fact, they hadn't had a winning season since 1986. But the 1993 team genuinely loved to play the game. They didn't look like a typical major league baseball team, like typical major league players. There was a considerable amount of hype about their appearance, how they were overweight and needed haircuts. Juan Guzman compared them to truck drivers, and the media took that to the extreme.

The reason Philadelphia seemed to be the people's favorite was that the players looked so unpolished. But the thing they did better than anybody else was play hard from the first pitch to the last, the way the game is supposed to be played.

The Phillies were impressive because they scored runs. I never saw John Kruk being overweight. I saw a guy who hit line drives. I never saw Dykstra as anything but a player who played hard and loved to play the game, and who constantly came up with clutch hits.

Philadelphia also played *smart* baseball. At the plate, they were patient all year. If they knew the pitcher wasn't going to be around the plate, they made him throw strikes. That's why they were successful against Dave Stewart in Game Two. In fact, they hit the ball well the entire Series, but they weren't always getting the timely hits. That's something that happens all the time in baseball, even with a good-hitting team, but it also clarifies how much better the Blue Jays were at hitting. If the Blue Jays and Phillies were hitting against the same pitching staff, the Blue Jays would have outscored them every day.

The Phillies were just one hit shy of winning Game Six. That was the only game during the Series that Philadelphia staged a comeback late in the game, scoring five times in the seventh to take a 6-5 lead. They needed at least one or two more runs and had runners on first and third with two outs in the seventh, but Kevin Stocker swung at three bad pitches and struck out. This isn't to criticize Stocker. It happens to everyone who hasn't had a lot of time in the big leagues, and Stocker was one of the youngest starting shortstops ever to play in a World Series.

That's another example of the stage becoming bigger the closer it gets to the fourth or fifth game. Players' fragilities become much more apparent. Stocker didn't have enough experience to know what to do with that situation. But he's a good, smart player. He'll learn from the experience. He's bound to have a great career, and hopefully he'll get another chance to play in the World Series.

Those are the things that decide winners and losers. Likewise, all the things before Joe Carter's home run set the stage for him to hit that home run. For example, in the eighth inning of Game Six, the Blue Jays had the middle of the order coming up: Carter, Olerud and Alomar against Larry Andersen. Had the Phillies retired the side in order, the bottom of the lineup would have been coming up in the ninth. Instead, Olerud walked, Fernandez was hit by a pitch, and Sprague walked to load the bases. Philadelphia didn't get out of the inning until Borders, the No. 9 hitter, popped out.

That meant the bottom of the ninth started with the top of the order, and Fregosi brought in Mitch Williams in a move that will be second-guessed forever.

Fregosi did the only thing he could. He didn't have a choice. What if he didn't use Williams in that situation? How would he use him next year if he didn't use him then? The point is, he *had* to use him. It was the natural thing to do. Fregosi stayed with his pattern of trying to get to Mitch to pitch the ninth once he got ahead. The other question is, if he didn't use Mitch Williams, then whom would he have used? Tommy Greene? You can't develop a new stopper in the sixth game of the World Series.

Mitch Williams has always pitched like that, right on the edge. During the season, he had been able to get out of the jams he made for himself. He would always come in, walk a guy, put another guy on. It would always take him some time to establish his rhythm. Then he'd get out of it. But the Blue Jays were a better team than he was used to seeing, and the best team will not let a pitcher off the hook when he makes mistakes.

That he walked Rickey on four straight pitches wasn't at all surprising. Rickey was going to make Williams throw three strikes, and it wasn't likely that Williams would throw three strikes. Once Rickey got on, the Blue Jays were in a great position at least to tie the game because he's so dangerous on the bases. Then Molitor got a hit, so there were two runners on with one out and Carter at the plate.

Usually, Carter will hook that ball foul. His swing is so quick and he gets in front of that kind of pitch. This time, he hit it so hard it didn't have time to hook.

From a purely human standpoint, it's hard not to feel sorry for Mitch Williams. He got branded with the label that he can't win the big game. That's neither true nor fair. Giving up the home run is unfortunate because he had to walk off the mound the way he did. Pro athletes, on a stage like the World Series, can be negatively affected for the rest of their lives by something they do. Dennis Eckersley could have been marked like that after he threw the home run pitch to Kirk Gibson in 1988, but Eckersley was able to bounce back and make people forget about it. Mitch Williams is going to have to do the same thing. Nobody is going to remember that he had 43 saves in 1993. They'll remember him for Game Six. He's going to have to prove that he's better than what happened in the 1993 World Series.

One play never wins or loses a game or a World Series, and that was reinforced in this Series. The 1993 World Series was about great individual performances and great, hard-nosed baseball by both teams. In many World Series, I just remember who won. This one, I'll think of great games and great players. I'll think of Molitor, Carter, Dykstra, Schilling, Williams, Alomar.

To me, they made it a Series to remember.

Fans—real and inanimate—
gather at SkyDome for
Toronto's second straight
World Series.

"I mean, it's just hair.
It grows on everyone."
—John Kruk

GAME ONE
October 16, at SkyDome

Although tension and drama await, the players are able to relax in the clubhouse before the game. Above, Toronto's Ed Sprague, John Olerud and Paul Molitor. Right, Philadelphia's Darren Daulton and Pete Incaviglia.

Top, Devon White and Dave Stewart.
Above, David West. Right, Joe Carter.

Left, equipment in hand, Jim Eisenreich is ready for the pre-game warmup. Below, Joe Carter. Bottom, Rickey Henderson.

31

Top, Paul Molitor. Above, batterymates Pat Borders and Duane Ward. Right, the Phanatic's uniform, big shoes and all, awaits its rightful owner. Opposite, Rickey Henderson at play with Dave Stewart.

Top, Mickey Morandini, Dave Hollins and Danny Jackson. Below, Joe Carter clowns with his teammates. Opposite, Joe Carter and Mitch Williams greet each other for the first time in the Series.

Top, Aretha Franklin starts the Series by singing the Star Spangled Banner. Bottom, left to right, Mariano Duncan, Ricky Jordan and Dave Stewart; Lenny Dykstra; the Blue Jays mascot; managers Cito Gaston and Jim Fregosi; the Phanatic and friend.

Above and right, Lenny Dykstra steals second after walking to lead off the game, and John Kruk drives him in with a single for the first run of the Series. Opposite, Juan Guzman.

Right, Paul Molitor and John Kruk. Below, John Olerud singles to left.

Devon White hits a fly ball to left, where a near-collision between Lenny Dykstra and Milt Thompson results in a dropped ball.

On back-to-back plays, Roberto Alomar makes a sensational grab off the bat of Lenny Dykstra in the fifth, and Rickey Henderson is unable to pull down Mariano Duncan's fly ball, which goes for a triple.

Opposite top, Duncan scores on a wild pitch. Bottom left, Manager Cito Gaston and Pat Borders talk with Juan Guzman. Bottom right, Ricky Jordan connects for a single.

Above, Jim Fregosi, obscured by Darren Daulton, takes the ball from Curt Schilling in the seventh. Left, Roberto Alomar slides into third with a stolen base.

Opposite, Milt Thompson goes against the wall to catch Paul Molitor's fly ball, ending Toronto's seventh-inning onslaught.

The Toronto fans, perhaps blasé over their team's second straight World Series appearance, were not exactly abuzz at Game One's outset. But there was plenty of electricity on the field as the two teams produced 21 hits and 13 runs. Tied 3-3 after three innings and 4-4 after five, the Blue Jays awakened the 52,011 at SkyDome (mischievously dubbed "ShyDome" by local columnists) with a three-run seventh thanks to four straight hits including back-to-back doubles by Devon White and Roberto Alomar. "Devo" and Robbie were the two main Toronto stars—White smashing a solo home run in the fifth and scoring three times, and Alomar making two sensational fielding plays—as the Blue Jays became the seventh straight home team to win the opening game of the Fall Classic.

TORONTO 8, PHILADELPHIA 5
Blue Jays lead Series, 1-0

GAME TWO

October 17, at SkyDome

Top, Devon White keeps the clubhouse attendants busy.
Left, Dave Stewart takes care of last-minute business.
Above, Curt Schilling, with the day off, relaxes.

Below, coach John Vukovich and Pete Incaviglia head out to the field. Right, Jim Eisenreich. Bottom, five Blue Jays in a private moment of team unity. Opposite, there's always room for a little pre-game fraternizing.

As the game draws nearer, attention turns to business. Above, even though SkyDome is climate-controlled, Cito Gaston refuses to take off his lucky Starter Blue Jays dugout jacket. Right, Joe Carter.

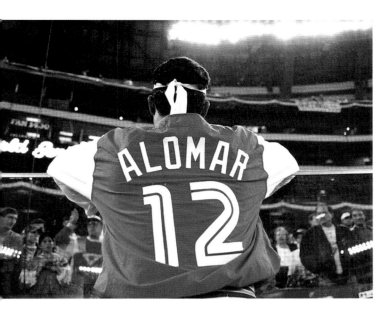

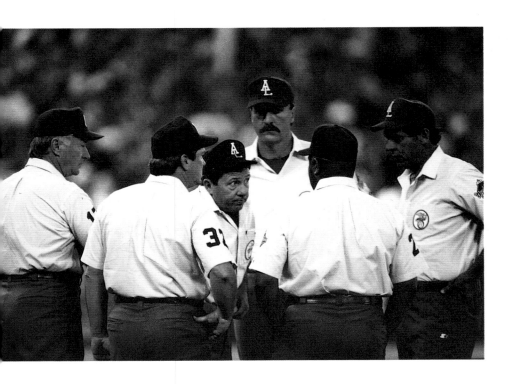

Above, perhaps the greatest thrill for a child at a World Series is to catch a baseball. Right, Toronto's Game Two starting pitcher, Dave Stewart. Below, Tony Fernandez tries to flag down a base hit, without success.

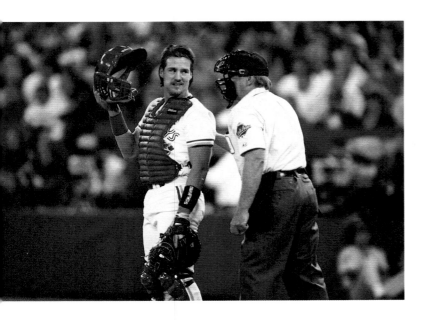

Top left, Pat Borders and home plate umpire Paul Runge. Top right, John Kruk and Roberto Alomar. Left, Terry Mulholland.

Top, a Roberto Alomar gonna-be. Right, Jim Eisenreich delivers Game Two's biggest hit, a three-run home run in the third.

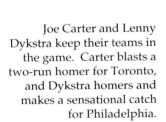

Joe Carter and Lenny Dykstra keep their teams in the game. Carter blasts a two-run homer for Toronto, and Dykstra homers and makes a sensational catch for Philadelphia.

Opposite, Curt Schilling can't stand the suspense as Mitch Williams collects the save. The World Series is played by adults, but baseball will always be a kid's game.

Opposite, Darren Daulton upends Tony Fernandez, who manages to complete the ninth-inning double play.

Above, Fernandez prevents Mariano Duncan from turning two in the ninth. Left and below, reporters dig for the inside story.

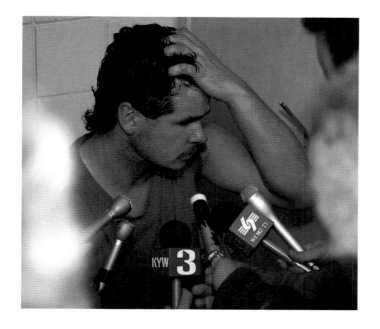

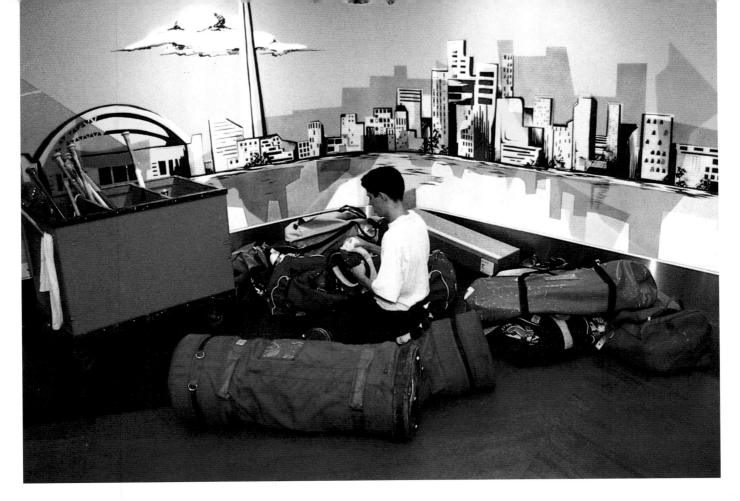

The Phillies pounced on Dave Stewart for five runs in the third after Stewart had walked the first two batters of the inning. The big blow—a three-run homer—came from an unlikely source, rightfielder Jim Eisenreich, who had hit only seven home runs all season. The Blue Jays, no strangers to comeback situations, gradually pecked away, narrowing their deficit to 5-3 before Lenny Dykstra provided a big run with a solo homer to lead off the seventh. Philadelphia starter Terry Mulholland, after bouncing his first pitch of the game in the dirt, comported himself extremely well before turning it over to Roger Mason and then Mitch Williams. The Blue Jays ran themselves out of what could have been a big threat when Williams caught Roberto Alomar on an attempted steal of third for the last out of the eighth.

PHILADELPHIA 6, TORONTO 4

Series tied, 1-1

Pre-game activity begins hours before the park opens.
Right, Juan Guzman works out by running in the stands.

"Paul Molitor
doesn't care about
his body. He just
wants to win."
   —Cito Gaston

GAME THREE

October 19, at Veterans Stadium

Top left, Jim Fregosi welcomes Cito Gaston to Philadelphia. In one of the Series' most provocative decisions, Gaston plays Paul Molitor at first base in place of American League batting champion John Olerud. Molitor singles, triples and homers and scores three times in the game. Roberto Alomar collected four of the Blue Jays' 13 hits, including a triple. Left, Danny Jackson.

Right, Tony Fernandez hops over Kevin Stocker and completes the double play. Middle, Lenny Dykstra checks the signs. Bottom right, Stocker takes a short-hop as Roberto Alomar steals the base. Below, Pat Hentgen. Opposite top, Rickey Henderson concentrates on the pitcher's delivery.

Right, Rickey Henderson hits a double to center. Below, Roberto Alomar steals third.

Opposite, clockwise from top left, Larry Andersen; Pat Borders; a home run by Milt Thompson; Alomar scoops up a grounder.

Steady rain that delayed the game by 72 minutes did nothing to warp the bats of the Blue Jays, whose first three batters scored against shaky southpaw Danny Jackson. The inning's big hit was a two-run triple by Paul Molitor, who solved Manager Cito Gaston's quandary resulting from the imposition of National League rules, which do not allow for a designated hitter. Gaston toyed with using Molitor, the Jays' regular DH, at third base, even though Molitor was unaccustomed to the position and also had a sore right shoulder. Gaston's gutsy decision: Bench American League batting champion John Olerud, a lefty, in favor of the right-handed Molitor at first base and keep Ed Sprague at third. Molitor collected three hits, including a solo homer in the third, scored three times, and started an important double play in the Phillies' seventh to snuff a serious threat.

TORONTO 10, PHILADELPHIA 3
Blue Jays lead Series, 2-1

GAME FOUR

October 20, at Veterans Stadium

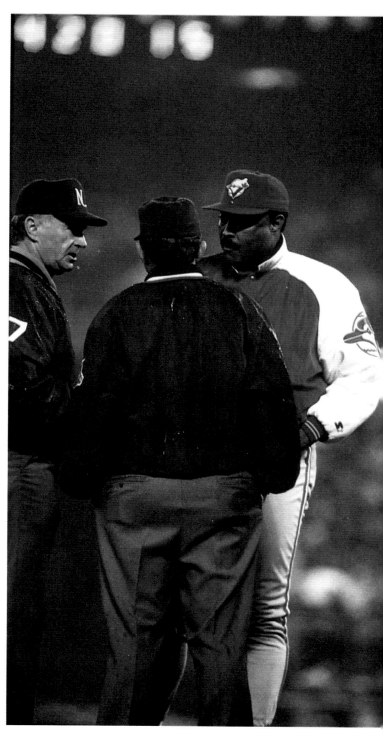

Above, Tommy Greene. Right, Paul Molitor plays third base for the first time since 1989. Far right, Joe Carter connects.

Opposite top, Carter's line drive rifles past Dave Hollins. Bottom right, Todd Stottlemyre is out at third—and bangs himself up—trying to advance from first on Roberto Alomar's seond-inning single.

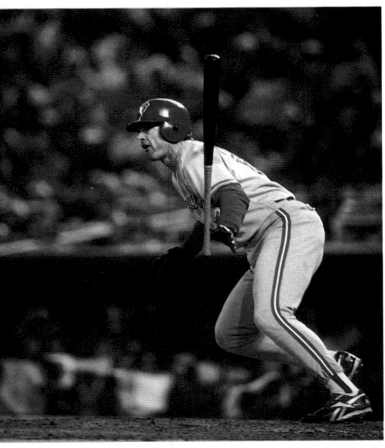

Top, John Kruk and John Olerud. Above left, Paul Molitor.
Opposite, steady rain can't put out the fire in
Lenny Dykstra's bat.

Top, Milt Thompson. Left, John Olerud's classy swing. Above, Jim Eisenreich laments a big one that got away.

Top, Paul Molitor rounds second and checks to see if the ball is still in play. Right, Dave Hollins doubles to center.

Left, Cito Gaston makes a point with Charlie Williams. Above, Mitch Williams.

| BLUE JAYS | 3 0 4 0 0 2 0 6 0 | 15 17 0 |
| PHILLIES | 4 2 0 15 1 1 0 | 14 14 1 |

The end of an epic battle. Top, Duane Ward. Above, congratulations all around.
Right, Cito Gaston and Pat Borders.
Opposite, clockwise from top left, Rickey Henderson; Mike Timlin; Todd
Stottlemyre with a bloody badge on his chin; Roberto Alomar.

A remarkable night and a remarkable game. Water poured from the skies, hits thundered from the bats and, when it was all over—four hours, 14 minutes and several Series records after it began—tears rained from the eyes of Phillies fans. The Blue Jays twice overcame five-run deficits—including a 14-9 bulge in the eighth inning—to win a game whose legend will only grow with every passing year. That Philadelphia scored 14 runs and lost—a Series record—was one thing; that Toronto scored 15 runs without the benefit of a home run was something else. The Blue Jays scored six times in the eighth for the win, with the tying and winning runs coming across on Devon White's triple to center. Lenny Dykstra slugged a pair of two-run homers and a double in a losing effort. Said Joe Carter: "Guys were going out there like it was a slo-pitch softball game." Paul Molitor played third base and handled the position flawlessly.

TORONTO 15, PHILADELPHIA 14
Blue Jays lead Series, 3-1

GAME FIVE

October 21, at Veterans Stadium

"Will pitch middle relief for food."
—Sign in the stands

Delayed from flying over the World Series, first by SkyDome's closed roof and then by Philadelphia's inclement weather, Bud One Airship finally lifts off for an evening above Veterans Stadium.

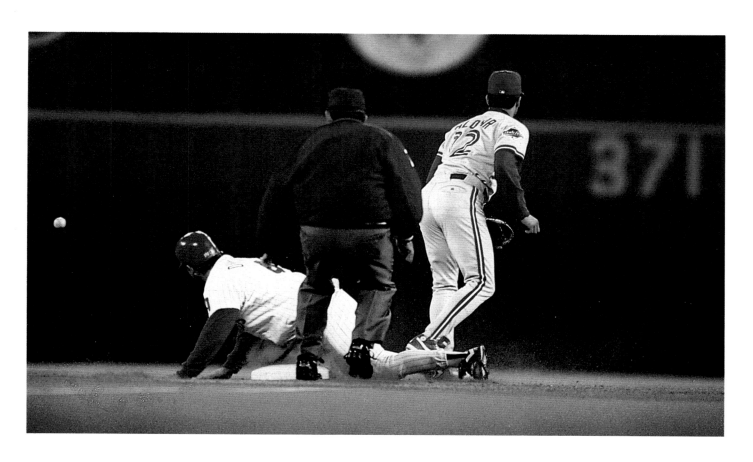

Opposite top, Juan Guzman. Opposite bottom, Lenny Dykstra avoids a pickoff attempt at first and, above, steals second. Left and below, Darren Daulton and Kevin Stocker double in the second for the game's final run.

Top, John Kruk.
Right, Jim Eisenreich.

Top, Curt Schilling with Rickey Henderson aboard. Right, Schilling lays down a sacrifice in the fourth.

Darren Daulton guns down Roberto Alomar, Mariano Duncan applying the tag. Opposite top, Duncan pulls back on a bunt. Bottom, John Kruk breaks the tension with Rickey Henderson and coach Bob Bailor before the action resumes.

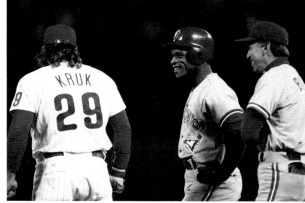

Right, Devon White. Opposite top,
Roberto Alomar gets back to first.

Above, Willie Canate, pinch-running at third base with nobody out in the eighth, gets caught in a pickle on an infield grounder. Darren Daulton runs him back to third and Dave Hollins tags him out. Below, Daulton congratulates Curt Schilling on his shutout victory, forcing a return to Toronto for Game Six.

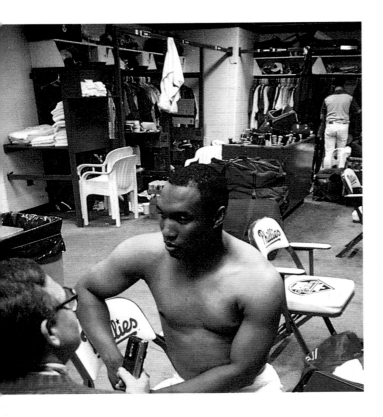

Needing to win, and especially needing a well-pitched game, Philadelphia turned to Curt Schilling. He responded with a masterful five-hit, complete game shutout and turned in an important defensive play in the eighth to send the Series back to Canada. This game was everything Game Four was not. The Phillies scratched across single runs in the first and second innings and managed only five hits themselves. Toronto's sluggers again hit some shots, but this time they died in the heavy air; the Blue Jays hit 10 fly-ball outs in the game. For the first time in the Series, the game was played in under three hours (2:53).

PHILADELPHIA 2, TORONTO 0
Blue Jays lead Series, 3-2

GAME SIX

October 23, at SkyDome

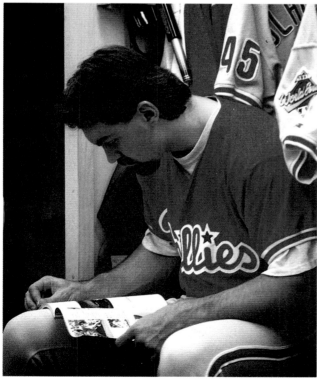

Left, Darren Daulton.
Opposite bottom, Mitch Williams.

Top, John Olerud rounds second
base after his first-inning double
and right, Roberto Alomar drives
him in with a single up the middle.

Left, Darren Daulton bloops a double in the fourth. Bottom, Pat Borders. Opposite, Dave Stewart.

122

Opposite, Milt Thompson watches Paul Molitor's MVP-clinching home run sail over the wall in the fourth. Top, Molitor passes third base coach Nick Leyva on his way home. Above, Terry Mulholland. Right, Al Leiter.

Lenny Dykstra hits his fourth home run of the Series in the seventh, well over the head of Joe Carter.

Top, Dave Hollins enjoys a hero's welcome after scoring in the seventh. Left, Larry Andersen and David West warm up in the bullpen. Above, Tony Fernandez gets hit by a pitch in the eighth.

Above, conference on the mound with Kim Batiste, John Kruk, Mitch Williams and Darren Daulton. Right, Williams looks for the sign. Opposite, Joe Carter hits the shot heard 'round Canada.

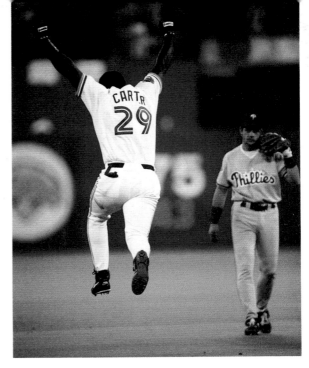

'You always hope it's you in that situation,' Joe Carter said. 'I still can't believe it went out.' Nor could the Phillies, the Blue Jays and the fans.

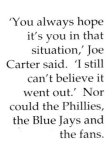

130

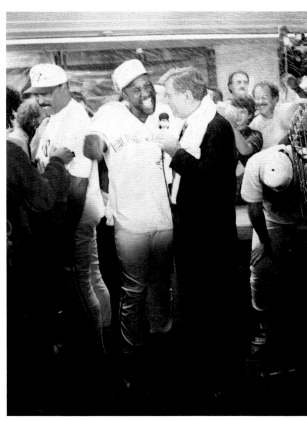

Back home in front of their eager fans, one victory from a second straight World Championship, the Blue Jays bolted to a 3-0 first-inning lead on a triple by Paul Molitor, a double by John Olerud and a single by Roberto Alomar. Toronto increased the bulge to 5-1 in the fifth as Molitor homered to left. But this one was far from over. Philadelphia scored five times in the seventh—Lenny Dykstra contributing the key hit with a dramatic three-run homer to right—to take a 6-5 lead. The Blue Jays loaded the bases in the eighth but came away empty-handed, setting up a ninth inning that would provide one of the greatest endings in World Series history. With Philadelphia's Mitch Williams pitching, Rickey Henderson walked on four straight pitches, Devon White flied out, Paul Molitor, the Series MVP, singled to center and Joe Carter rocketed a line-drive over the left-field wall. Seemingly stunned for half a second before fully realizing what had just unfolded, Canada rose up as one and roared. Again.

TORONTO 8, PHILADELPHIA 6
Blue Jays win Series, 4-2

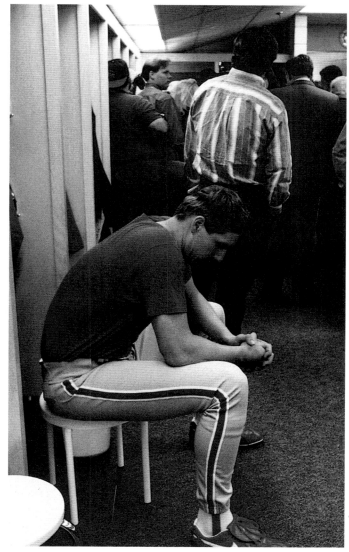

Opposite top, Rickey Henderson and Joe Carter join in the traditional champagne celebration. Above, dejection descends upon the Phillies. Middle, Dave Stewart. Right, Mitch Williams ponders his place in history.

Left, Paul Molitor shows off his MVP trophy to CBS' Tim McCarver and the world. Below, Buck Martinez interviews Molitor for TSN. Bottom, the fans get a taste of the bubbly. Opposite top, the players' celebration spreads to the field. Opposite bottom, Molitor and Joe Carter salute the crowd.

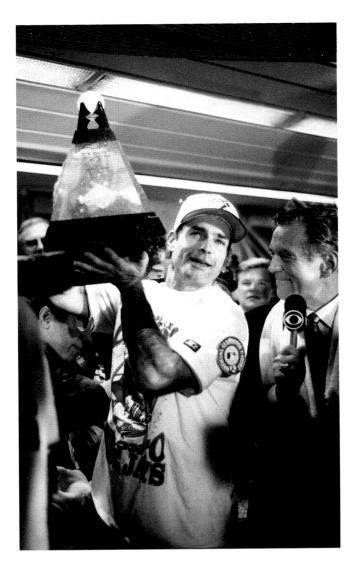

Top, Rickey Henderson and Joe Carter with the World Series Trophy. Opposite, the fans' celebration begins.

136

Top left, Juan Guzman and Roberto Alomar.
Upper left, Paul Molitor signs a glove. Lower
left, Danny Cox acknowledges the cheers.
Bottom left, Pat Borders and family.

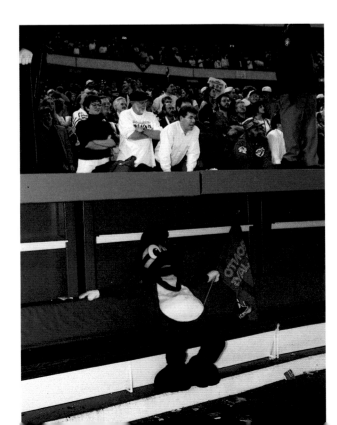

Opposite top, Joe Carter. Middle left, Rickey Henderson and Dave Stewart. Middle right, Devon White. Left and below, White and Roberto Alomar thank the fans.

THE WORLD SERIES IN NUMBERS

GAME ONE

Philadelphia	ab	r	h	bi
Dykstra, cf	4	1	1	0
Duncan, 2b	5	2	3	0
Kruk, 1b	4	2	3	2
Hollins, 3b	4	0	0	0
Daulton, c	4	0	1	1
Eisenreich, rf	5	0	1	1
Jordan, dh	5	0	1	0
Thompson, lf	3	0	0	0
Incaviglia, ph-lf	1	0	0	0
Stocker, ss	3	0	1	0
	38	5	11	4
Toronto	ab	r	h	bi
Henderson, lf	3	1	1	0
White, cf	4	3	2	2
Alomar, 2b	4	0	1	2
Carter, rf	3	1	1	1
Olerud, 1b	3	2	2	1
Molitor, dh	4	0	1	1
Fernandez, ss	3	0	0	1
Sprague, 3b	4	0	1	0
Borders, c	4	1	1	0
	32	8	10	8

Philadelphia	201	010	001 — 5
Toronto	021	011	30x — 8

E—Thompson; Alomar, Sprague, Carter. DP—Philadelphia 1; Toronto 1. LOB—Philadelphia 11, Toronto 4. HR—White (1) off Schilling in the 5th, 0 on; Olerud (1) off Schilling in the 6th, 0 on. S B—Dykstra (1), Duncan (1); Alomar (1). CS—Fernandez. SF—Carter (off Schilling).

Philadelphia	IP	H	R	ER	BB	SO
Schilling L, 0-1	6.1	8	7	6	2	3
West	0	2	1	1	0	0
Andersen	0.2	0	0	0	1	1
Mason	1	0	0	0	0	1
Toronto						
Guzman	5	5	4	4	4	6
Leiter W, 1-0	2.2	4	0	0	1	2
Ward S, 1	1.1	2	1	0	0	3

WP—Guzman. PB—Daulton. T—3:27. A—52,011.

GAME TWO

Philadelphia	ab	r	h	bi
Dykstra, cf	4	2	2	1
Duncan, 2b	4	1	1	0
Kruk, 1b	5	1	2	1
Hollins, 3b	4	1	2	1
Batiste, 3b	0	0	0	0
Daulton, c	5	0	1	0
Eisenreich, rf	4	1	1	3
Incaviglia, lf	4	0	1	0
Thompson, pr-lf	0	0	0	0
Jordan, dh	4	0	1	0
Stocker, ss	3	0	1	0
	37	6	12	6
Toronto	ab	r	h	bi
Henderson, lf	3	0	0	0
White, cf	4	0	1	0
Molitor, dh	3	2	2	0
Carter, rf	4	1	1	2
Olerud, 1b	3	0	0	1
Alomar, 2b	3	1	1	0
Fernandez, ss	3	0	2	1
Sprague, 3b	4	0	0	0
Griffin, pr	0	0	0	0
Borders, c	4	0	1	0
	31	4	8	4

Philadelphia	005	000	100 — 6
Toronto	000	201	010 — 4

DP—Philadelphia 1; Toronto 1. LOB—Philadelphia 9, Toronto 5. HR—Eisenreich (1) off Stewart in the 3rd, 2 on; Carter (1) off Mulholland in the 4th, 1 on; Dykstra (1) off Castillo in the 7th, 0 on. SB—Molitor (1), Alomar (2). CS—Henderson, Alomar; Stocker. SF—Olerud (off Williams).

Philadelphia	IP	H	R	ER	BB	SO
Mulholland W, 1-0	5.2	7	3	3	2	4
Mason	1.2	1	1	1	0	2
Williams S, 1	1.2	0	0	0	2	0
Toronto						
Stewart L, 0-1	6	6	5	5	4	6
Castillo	1	3	1	1	0	0
Eichhorn	0.1	1	0	0	1	0
Timlin	1.2	2	0	0	0	2

WP—Stewart. Balk—Stewart. T—3:35. A—52,062.

GAME THREE

Toronto	ab	r	h	bi
Henderson, lf	4	2	2	0
White, cf	4	2	1	1
Molitor, 1b	4	3	3	3
Carter, rf	4	1	1	1
Alomar, 2b	5	2	4	2
Fernandez, ss	3	0	2	2
Sprague, 3b	4	0	0	1
Borders, c	4	0	0	0
Hentgen, p	3	0	0	0
Cox, p	1	0	0	0
Ward, p	0	0	0	0
	36	10	13	10
Philadelphia	ab	r	h	bi
Dykstra, cf	5	0	1	0
Duncan, 2b	5	0	2	1
Kruk, 1b	3	1	2	0
Hollins, 3b	3	0	0	0
Daulton, c	3	0	0	0
Eisenreich, rf	4	0	1	1
Incaviglia, lf	3	0	0	0
Thigpen, p	0	0	0	0
Morandini, ph	0	0	0	0
Andersen, p	0	0	0	0
Stocker, ss	4	0	1	0
Jackson, p	1	0	0	0
Chamberlain, ph	1	0	0	0
Rivera, p	0	0	0	0
Thompson, lf	2	2	2	1
	34	3	9	3

Toronto	301	001	302 — 10
Philadelphia	000	001	101 — 3

E—Carter. DP—Toronto 2. LOB—Toronto 7, Philadelphia 9. HR—Molitor (1) off Jackson in the 3rd, 0 on; Thompson (1) off Ward in the 9th, 0 on. SB—Alomar 2 (4). SF—Carter (off Jackson), Fernandez (off Rivera), Sprague (off Thigpen).

Toronto	IP	H	R	ER	BB	SO
Hentgen W, 1-0	6	5	1	1	3	6
Cox	2	3	1	1	2	2
Ward	1	1	1	1	0	2
Philadelphia						
Jackson L, 0-1	5	6	4	4	1	1
Rivera	1.1	4	4	4	2	3
Thigpen	1.2	0	0	0	1	0
Andersen	1	3	2	2	0	0

HBP—by Thigpen (Henderson). T—3:16. A—62,689.

TORONTO BLUE JAYS

Batting

PLAYER	AVG	G	AB	R	H	TB	2B	3B	HR	RBI	BB	SO	SB
Alomar	.480	6	25	5	12	16	2	1	0	6	2	3	4
Borders	.304	6	23	2	7	7	0	0	1	2	1	0	0
Butler	.500	2	2	1	1	1	0	0	0	0	0	0	0
Canate	.000	1	0	0	0	0	0	0	0	0	0	0	0
Carter	.280	6	25	6	7	14	1	0	2	8	0	4	0
Coles	.000	0	0	0	0	0	0	0	0	0	0	0	0
Fernandez	.333	6	21	2	7	8	1	0	0	9	3	3	0
Griffin	.000	3	0	0	0	0	0	0	0	0	0	0	0
Henderson	.227	6	22	6	5	7	2	0	0	2	5	2	1
Knorr	.000	1	0	0	0	0	0	0	0	0	0	0	0
Molitor	.500	6	24	10	12	24	2	2	2	8	3	0	1
Olerud	.235	5	17	5	4	8	1	0	1	2	4	1	0
Schofield	.000	0	0	0	0	0	0	0	0	0	0	0	0
Sprague	.067	5	15	0	1	1	0	0	0	2	1	6	0
White	.292	6	24	8	7	17	3	2	1	7	4	7	1
Castillo	.000	2	1	0	0	0	0	0	0	0	0	1	0
Cox	.000	3	1	0	0	0	0	0	0	0	0	0	0
Guzman	.000	2	2	0	0	0	0	0	0	0	0	0	0
Hentgen	.000	1	3	0	0	0	0	0	0	0	0	1	0
Leiter	1.000	3	1	0	1	2	1	0	0	0	0	0	0
Stottlemyre	.000	1	0	0	0	0	0	0	0	0	0	0	0
TOTALS	.311	6	206	45	64	105	13	5	6	45	25	30	7

Pitching

PITCHER	W	L	ERA	G	GS	IP	H	R	ER	HR	BB	SO
Castillo	1	0	8.10	2	0	3.1	6	3	3	1	3	1
Cox	0	0	8.10	3	0	3.1	6	3	3	0	5	6
Eichhorn	0	0	0.00	1	0	0.1	1	0	0	0	1	0
Guzman	0	1	3.75	2	2	12.0	10	6	5	0	8	12
Hentgen	1	0	1.50	1	1	6.0	5	1	1	0	3	6
Leiter	1	0	7.71	3	0	7.0	12	6	6	2	2	5
Stewart	0	1	6.75	2	2	12.0	10	9	9	2	8	8
Stottlemyre	0	0	27.00	1	1	2.0	3	6	6	1	4	1
Timlin	0	0	0.00	2	0	2.1	2	0	0	0	0	4
Ward	1	0	1.93	4	0	4.2	3	2	1	1	0	7
TOTALS	4	2	5.77	6	6	53.0	58	36	34	7	34	50

Complete games—None. Saves—Ward 2.

Compiled by the MLB-IBM Baseball Information System.
© Copyright 1993 MLB.

THE WORLD SERIES IN NUMBERS

GAME FOUR

Toronto	ab	r	h	bi
Henderson, lf	5	2	2	2
White, cf	5	2	3	4
Alomar, 2b	6	1	2	1
Carter, rf	6	2	3	0
Olerud, 1b	4	2	1	0
Molitor, 3b	4	2	2	2
Griffin, 3b	0	0	0	0
Fernandez, ss	6	2	3	5
Borders, c	4	1	1	1
Stottlemyre, p	0	0	0	0
Butler, ph	1	1	0	0
Leiter, p	1	0	1	0
Castillo, p	1	0	0	0
Sprague, ph	1	0	0	0
Timlin, p	0	0	0	0
Ward, p	0	0	0	0
	44	15	18	15
Philadelphia	**ab**	**r**	**h**	**bi**
Dykstra, cf	5	4	3	4
Duncan, 2b	6	1	3	1
Kruk, 1b	5	0	0	0
Hollins, 3b	4	3	2	0
Daulton, c	3	2	1	3
Eisenreich, rf	4	2	1	1
Thompson, lf	5	1	3	5
Stocker, ss	4	0	0	0
Greene, p	1	1	1	0
Mason, p	1	0	0	0
Jordan, ph	1	0	0	0
West, p	0	0	0	0
Chamberlain, ph	1	0	0	0
Andersen, p	0	0	0	0
Williams, p	0	0	0	0
Morandini, ph	1	0	0	0
Thigpen, p	0	0	0	0
	41	14	14	14

Toronto   3 0 4   0 0 2   0 6 0 — 15
Philadelphia   4 2 0   1 5 1   1 0 0 — 14

LOB—Toronto 10, Philadelphia 8. HR—Dykstra 2 (3) off Stottlemyre in the 2nd, 1 on, off Leiter in the 5th, 1 on; Daulton (1) off Leiter in the 5th, 1 on. SB—Henderson (1), White (1); Dykstra (2), Duncan (2).

Toronto	IP	H	R	ER	BB	SO
Stottlemyre	2	3	6	6	4	1
Leiter	2.2	8	6	6	0	1
Castillo W, 1-0	2.1	3	2	2	3	1
Timlin	0.2	0	0	0	0	2
Ward S, 2	1.1	0	0	0	0	2
Philadelphia						
Greene	2.1	7	7	7	4	1
Mason	2.2	2	0	0	1	2
West	1	3	2	2	0	0
Andersen	1.1	2	3	3	1	2
Williams L, 0-1	0.2	3	3	3	1	1
Thigpen	1	1	0	0	0	0

HBP—by Castillo (Daulton); by West (Molitor). T—4:14. A—62,731.

GAME FIVE

Toronto	ab	r	h	bi
Henderson, lf	3	0	0	0
White, cf	3	0	0	0
Alomar, 2b	3	0	1	0
Carter, rf	4	0	0	0
Olerud, 1b	4	0	0	0
Molitor, 3b	4	0	1	0
Fernandez, ss	3	0	0	0
Borders, c	3	0	2	0
Canate, pr	0	0	0	0
Knorr, c	0	0	0	0
Guzman, p	2	0	0	0
Butler, ph	1	0	1	0
Cox, p	0	0	0	0
	30	0	5	0
Philadelphia	**ab**	**r**	**h**	**bi**
Dykstra, cf	2	1	0	0
Duncan, 2b	4	0	0	0
Kruk, 1b	3	0	1	1
Hollins, 3b	3	0	1	0
Batiste, 3b	0	0	0	0
Daulton, c	4	1	1	0
Eisenreich, rf	4	0	0	0
Thompson, lf	3	0	0	0
Stocker, ss	2	0	1	1
Schilling, p	2	0	1	0
	27	2	5	2

Toronto   0 0 0   0 0 0   0 0 0 — 0
Philadelphia   1 1 0   0 0 0   0 0 x — 2

E—Borders; Duncan. DP—Toronto 1; Philadelphia 3. LOB—Toronto 6, Philadelphia 8. SB—Dykstra (3). CS—Alomar. S—Schilling (off Guzman).

Toronto	IP	H	R	ER	BB	SO
Guzman L, 0-1	7	5	2	1	4	6
Cox	1	0	0	0	2	3
Philadelphia						
Schilling W, 1-1	9	5	0	0	3	6

T—2:53. A—62,706.

GAME SIX

Philadelphia	ab	r	h	bi
Dykstra, cf	3	1	1	3
Duncan, dh	5	1	1	0
Kruk, 1b	3	0	0	0
Hollins, 3b	5	1	1	1
Batiste, 3b	0	0	0	0
Daulton, c	4	1	1	0
Eisenreich, rf	5	0	2	1
Thompson, lf	3	0	0	0
Incaviglia, ph-lf	0	0	0	1
Stocker, ss	3	1	0	0
Morandini, 2b	4	1	1	0
	35	6	7	6
Toronto	**ab**	**r**	**h**	**bi**
Henderson, lf	4	1	0	0
White, cf	4	1	0	0
Molitor, dh	5	3	3	2
Carter, rf	4	1	1	4
Olerud, 1b	3	1	1	0
Griffin, pr-3b	0	0	0	0
Alomar, 2b	4	1	3	1
Fernandez, ss	3	0	0	0
Sprague, 3b-1b	2	0	0	1
Borders, c	4	0	2	0
	33	8	10	8

Philadelphia   0 0 0   1 0 0   5 0 0 — 6
Toronto   3 0 0   1 1 0   0 0 3 — 8

One out when winning run scored.
E—Alomar, Sprague. LOB—Philadelphia 9, Toronto 7. HR—Molitor (2) off Mulholland in the 5th, 0 on; Dykstra (4) off Stewart in the 7th, 2 on; Carter (2) off Williams in the 9th, 2 on. SB—Duncan (3), Dykstra (4). SF—Incaviglia (off Leiter); Carter (off Mulholland), Sprague (off Mulholland).

Philadelphia	IP	H	R	ER	BB	SO
Mulholland	5	7	5	5	1	1
Mason	2.1	1	0	0	0	2
West	0	0	0	0	1	0
Andersen	0.2	0	0	0	1	0
Williams L, 0-2	0.1	2	3	3	1	0
Toronto						
Stewart	6	4	4	4	4	2
Cox	0.1	3	2	2	1	1
Leiter	1.2	0	0	0	1	2
Ward W, 1-0	1	0	0	0	0	0

Stewart pitched to 3 batters in the 7th. West pitched to one batter in the 8th.
HBP—by Andersen (Fernandez). T—3:27. A—52,195.

PHILADELPHIA PHILLIES

Batting

PLAYER	AVG	G	AB	R	H	TB	2B	3B	HR	RBI	BB	SO	SB
Batiste	.000	3	0	0	0	0	0	0	0	0	0	0	0
Chamberlain	.000	2	2	0	0	0	0	0	0	0	0	1	0
Daulton	.217	6	23	4	5	10	2	0	1	4	4	5	0
Duncan	.345	6	29	5	10	12	0	1	0	2	1	7	3
Dykstra	.348	6	23	9	8	21	1	0	4	8	7	4	4
Eisenreich	.231	6	26	3	6	9	0	0	1	7	2	4	0
Hollins	.261	6	23	5	6	7	1	0	0	2	6	5	0
Incaviglia	.125	4	8	0	1	1	0	0	0	1	0	4	0
Jordan	.200	3	10	2	2	2	0	0	0	0	0	2	0
Kruk	.348	6	23	4	8	9	1	0	0	4	7	7	0
Longmire	.000	0	0	0	0	0	0	0	0	0	0	0	0
Morandini	.200	3	5	1	1	1	0	0	0	0	1	2	0
Pratt	.000	0	0	0	0	0	0	0	0	0	0	0	0
Stocker	.211	6	19	1	4	5	1	0	0	1	5	5	0
Thompson	.313	6	16	3	5	11	1	1	1	6	1	2	0
Greene	1.000	1	1	1	1	1	0	0	0	0	0	0	0
Jackson	.000	1	1	0	0	0	0	0	0	0	0	1	0
Mason	.000	4	1	0	0	0	0	0	0	0	0	0	0
Schilling	.500	2	2	0	1	1	0	0	0	0	0	1	0
TOTALS	.274	6	212	36	58	90	7	2	7	35	34	50	7

Pitching

PITCHER	W	L	ERA	G	GS	IP	H	R	ER	HR	BB	SO
Andersen	0	0	12.27	4	0	3.2	5	5	5	0	3	3
Greene	0	0	27.00	1	1	2.1	7	7	7	0	4	1
Jackson	0	1	7.20	1	1	5.0	6	4	4	1	1	1
Mason	0	0	1.17	4	0	7.2	4	1	1	0	1	7
Mulholland	1	0	6.75	2	2	10.2	14	8	8	2	3	5
Rivera	0	0	27.00	1	0	1.1	4	4	4	0	2	3
Schilling	1	1	3.52	2	2	15.1	13	7	6	2	5	9
Thigpen	0	0	0.00	2	0	2.2	1	0	0	1	0	1
West	0	0	27.00	3	0	1.0	5	3	3	0	1	0
Williams	0	2	20.25	3	0	2.2	5	6	6	1	4	1
TOTALS	2	4	7.39	6	6	52.1	64	45	44	6	25	30

Complete games—Schilling 1. Saves—Williams 1.

Umpires—Dana DeMuth, Mark Johnson, Tim McClelland, Dave Phillips, Paul Runge, Charlie Williams.

A SERIES TO REMEMBER
CREATIVE STAFF

Top, left to right: David Lilienstein, Jon Rochmis, Laurence Hyman, Mickey Palmer, Jerry Wachter. Bottom, left to right: Michael Zagaris, Stephen Green, Beth Hansen, Jon Winet.

JOE MORGAN, of Danville, California, collected 2,517 hits and 689 stolen bases during his 22-year major league career. He was inducted into the Baseball Hall of Fame in 1990. Morgan, a baseball broadcaster since 1985, is a member of ESPN's primary play-by-play team. His biography, *JOE MORGAN: A Life in Baseball,* was released in the summer of 1993.

BUCK MARTINEZ, of Valley Village, California, played in the major leagues for 17 seasons, including seven as a Toronto Blue Jays catcher. Martinez has been an analyst on Toronto's TSN telecasts since 1987 and also works with ESPN. He has authored two books, *From Worst to First* (1985) and *The Last Out* (1986).

LAURENCE J. HYMAN, of San Francisco, is founder and president of Woodford Publishing, Inc., and publisher and creative director of Woodford Press. He was art director and designer of *A SERIES FOR THE WORLD* and *A SERIES TO REMEMBER.*

JON ROCHMIS, of Oakland, California, is editor at Woodford Press and Woodford Publishing, and a former Bay Area sportswriter.

DENNIS DESPROIS, of Scottsdale, Arizona, was editor of photography for *A SERIES FOR THE WORLD* and *A SERIES TO REMEMBER.*

JIM SANTORE, of Pleasant Hill, California, is art director at Woodford Publishing.

DAVID LILIENSTEIN, of San Francisco, is marketing director at Woodford Publishing and a free-lance photographer.

STEPHEN GREEN, of Chicago, was the photography crew chief for *A SERIES FOR THE WORLD* and *A SERIES TO REMEMBER.* He is the team photographer for the Chicago Cubs.

JON BLACKER, of Toronto, is a free-lance photographer and frequent contributor to *The Sporting News.*

BETH HANSEN, of San Francisco, is a free-lance photographer and graphic designer.

MARK O'NEILL, of Toronto, is a free-lance photographer.

MICKEY PALMER, of Staten Island, New York, is chief photographer for Major League Baseball's Office of the Commissioner. He owns Focus on Sports, one of the world's largest sports stock photography agencies.

ROSEMARY RAHN, of Philadelphia, is a team photographer for the Philadelphia Phillies.

JERRY WACHTER, of Baltimore, is team photographer for the Baltimore Orioles.

JON WINET, of Berkeley, California, is an artist, photographer and curator. His work has been exhibited in Moscow, New York, Chicago and Los Angeles.

MICHAEL ZAGARIS, of San Francisco, is known world-wide for his Rock-and-Roll photography. He is team photographer for the Oakland Athletics and San Francisco 49ers.

A SERIES TO REMEMBER: Toronto and Philadelphia, 1993, is Major League Baseball's official book of the World Series. This book represents the second in a series, and third overall, of official World Series books published by Woodford Press of San Francisco in partnership with Major League Baseball. Previous official World Series books were *THREE WEEKS IN OCTOBER,* the story of the 1989 "earthquake" World Series between the Oakland Athletics and San Francisco Giants, and *A SERIES FOR THE WORLD: Baseball's First International Fall Classic,* a chronicle of the 1992 World Series between Toronto and Atlanta. *A SERIES TO REMEMBER* was released five weeks following Game Six. More than 30,000 full-color slides were taken by 10 photographers, 350 of which were used. The text typeface used in this book is Palatino. Color separations were done by Riverside Scans of Sacramento, Calif., and printing and binding were done by Rand-McNally of Indianapolis, Ind.

PHOTOGRAPHY CREDITS

Jon Blacker: 22; 25 BL; 26 BL; 28 TR, M, B; 115 B; 139 BL; 140 TR, ML, MR; 141 B.

Stephen Green: 2-3; 11; 16; 30 BL; 32 BR; 34 T; 35; 40 T; 41 B; 43 T; 45 T; 47 TL; 49 BR; 50 TR, TL; 51 BR; 52 T; 53 TL; 54 TL; 56 B; 59 BL; 60 T; 61 T; 71 B; 73 BL; 75 A; 76 BL; 80 T; 91 R; 100 T, BL; 111 B; 113; 117 BL; 123 T; 125 BL, BR; 129; 131 B; 133 L, BR; 135 TR; 136 T.

Beth Hansen: 6-7; 8; 14; 15; 17; 24 B; 27 B; 38 B; 42 TL; 46 BL; 47 B; 48 A; 53 B; 54 B; 58 TL, ML; 62 BR; 64 B; 65 T, BL; 67 MR; 70 B; 71 TL, TR, MR; 72 A; 73 T; 80 L, M, R; 81 TL, TR; 82 TL, TR; 85 TL, BL; 90 ML, BL; 93 TR; 96 BL, BR; 97 A; 98 T; 99 T; 100 BR; 110 L; 116 TR; 118 B; 119 TR, B; 120 B; 123 B; 133 T; 137 B.

David Lilienstein: 23 T; 26 T; 46 T; 56-57; 57 T; 61 BR; 64 T; 68 BL; 73 BR; 83 TR, B; 85 TML, BML; 100 MR; 102 A; 103 A; 114 BR; 115 TR; 116 MR, B; 127 B; 131 T; 139 TL, upper L, lower L, BR; 140 TL; 141 TL, TR.

Mark O'Neill: 138 B; 139 TR.

Mickey Palmer: 36 L; 37 M, R; 40 B; 41 T; 43 BL, BR; 46 BR; 51 T; 55 TR; 57 B; 58 TR; 59 T; 68-69 T; 74 B; 76 TL; 78 B; 79 BR; 84 T; 85 R; 86 A; 88 BL; 89; 90 TL, BR; 91 T; 92 A; 93 BR; 94 T; 101 T; 104 T; 105 T, BL; 107 T; 108 B; 110 TR; 111 T; 122 T; 125 T; 134 TL.

Rosemary Rahn: 63 A.

Jerry Wachter: 1; 4-5; 36-37 T; 38 T; 39 T; 42 TR, B; 44 A; 55 B; 56 TL, TR; 58 B; 59 BR; 60 B, BL; 69 BL; 74 TL, TR; 76 MR, BR; 77 A; 79 TL, TR, BL; 87 T, BR; 88 T, BR; 90 TR; 91 B; 93 L; 94 BR; 105 BR; 106 T; 107 B; 108 TL, TR; 109 A; 110 B; 112 TL, TR, ML, B; 120 T; 121 A; 122 B; 126 A; 127 T, R; 128 TL; 130 TR; 134 TR, B; 135 TL, BR.

Jon Winet: 12; 18; 19; 20; 23 M, B; 24 T; 25 T; 26 BR; 27 T; 28 TL; 36-37 B; 40-41; 47 TR; 53 TR, ML, MR; 55 TL; 61 M, BL; 62 T, BL; 65 BR; 66 A; 67 TL, TR, ML, B; 68 BR; 69 BR; 70 T; 81 B; 82 B; 83 TL; 84 B; 96 T; 98 B; 99 B; 106 L; 114 BL; 115 TL; 116 TL, BL; 118 T; 119 MR; 132 BL, BR; 136 L; 137 T; 138 T; 140 BR, BL.

Michael Zagaris: 25 BR; 29 A; 30 T, BR; 31 A; 32 T, BL; 33; 34 B; 36 M; 39 B; 45 B; 49 T, BL; 50 T; 51 BL; 52 BL, BR; 54 TR; 76 TR; 78 T; 87 BL; 94 BL; 95 A; 104 B; 106 B; 112 MR; 114 TL, TR; 117 TL, R; 119 TL; 124; 128 R, BL; 130 TL, B; 132 TL, TR; 133 MR; 135 BL.

KEY: T=top; B=bottom; L=left; R=right; M=middle; A=all.